ONENOTE

Now with 125 tips and tricks to make you a OneNote expert

Table of Contents

Introduction

Thank you for downloading this book. If you have than it should be safe to assume that you either have or are going to download OneNote. If you have downloaded OneNote and you're having a difficult time wrapping your head around it, than this book is perfect for you. And if you haven't downloaded OneNote, and you're trying to decide if it's worth using, than this book is also perfect for you.

This book comes in two main sections. The first, is an outline of what OneNote is and how to use it. This is for the absolute beginner. It covers everything from setting up your first notebook to basic formatting, all the while highlight the benefits of using OneNote over other writing and note taking software,

The second section is for the slightly more experienced user who wants to take their OneNote skills to the next level. In this section not only do I cover new features and add-ons that you may not be aware of, but I will also provide 125 useful tips and tricks that you can do using your OneNote. These vary from the simple act of 'searching for tags,' to the far more complex and unique 'pulling text from an image,' and everything in between.

The great thing about this book is that it extends beyond a single read use. This is the kind of book that you will keep by your computer side at all times, already ready to look into and utilize when using

OneNote. I promise that if you do that, and apply the tips and tricks correctly, you will come out the other end a master of OneNote.

So don't put it off any longer, continue reading to see how you will become a master of OneNote.

Chapter One: The Brief

What is OneNote

Put simply, OneNote is a digital version of a notebook. Rather than having to carry around an actual, physical notebook full of cumbersome pages, binders and printouts all of which will inevitably get jumbled and mixed up, OneNote acts as an electronic version of this. Plain and simple.

But really it's so much more than that. OneNote is the future of note taking and organisational thinking to be used by everyone from students to stay at home parents.

The best way to think about OneNote is quite literally to picture it as a digital notepad. Once you have this in mind, you can start laying out and discovering the key benefits of using OneNote over an actual pad and pen. They're all digitally motivated and they're all designed to save you time and energy.

Say you're in a lecture and you don't feel like writing all the teachers notes down? With OneNote you can take a photo of the whiteboard and digitally insert it into your notes. Or say that your teacher is speaking endlessly and again you don't want to take notes? Simply audio-record the teacher, upload it to OneNote and then listen later – using OneNote's search function to find the key points you're looking for.

And those examples are only the beginning. It's online platform and simple layout design means that it quiet literally has infinite storing capabilities, all the while ensuring that you won't, and can't, lose your hard worked on notes.

However, it's hard, and almost impossible, to describe what OneNote is and what it's capabilities are without going into greater examples and breaking down its key functions. So read on to find out more about this amazing platform.

How it Differs From Word

This is definitely the most common question asked when it comes to OneNote. True, on the surface they seem rather similar. OneNote is after all just a blank page template to take notes on. Isn't that all Word is?

The only real similarity between the two is that they both open as blank pieces of paper that can be typed on. That's literally where it ends.

The first place where OneNote separates itself is its organisational merits. When you open a Word doc, you are presented with a blank page. As you type that page becomes two, then three and so on. If you're twenty pages down and want to find something that you wrote two hours ago you will need to scroll up and hope to god that you find it.

OneNote was designed to ensure that this kind of thing doesn't happen. It has a unique Notebook, Section and Page layout system which allows for you to separate and store notes as you see fit, based on your own criteria. It also has a search function that makes it super easy to find notes much later.

But that's just for basic note taking. OneNote allows for the user to upload everything from videos to JPEG images. These can be moved from pages to page and section to section. The user can constantly fiddle with the order of their notes, moving and rearranging as new information is found. The user can draw on their notes, choose templates and layouts designed for them and even share their notes online with other users – with both users editing the same notes, from different devices in real time.

OneNote's capabilities stops at your imagination. When it comes to taking and sharing notes, OneNote can do it all.

Multiple Platforms

One of the key components of OneNote 2016 is that it is now accessible entirely online. It is opened and operated through your web browser while everything gets updated and stored automatically into OneDrive. The advantage of this that, where once you would be bound to a single device when using OneNote, you can now have it spread across multiple devices.

OneNote is available on you PC, Mac, tablet, Iphone, Ipad, Android, IOS and indeed any 'smart' device that has online capabilities. What this ultimately means is that your OneNote usage is no longer bound to the device you have it downloaded onto. As long as you have internet access you can access your notebook and update your notes knowing that they are saved and secured.

To Pay Or Not?

There are currently two versions of OneNote on the market. They are OneNote 2016 Office and just plain old OneNote2016. The key difference is that Office costs money to download and install, where the other is free.

In my opinion there is almost no need to pay for the Office version. The only real difference is the online capabilities. The free version is exclusively regulated to OneDrive. The Officer version allows for the user to save their work to a local dropbox as well as OneDrive.

And that's about it. I would highly recommend using the free version, the differences aren't worth the cost.

Chapter Two: Getting Started

*A quick note. It should be pointed out that I will be addressing the user under the assumption that they are using OneNote for Windows.

The Basics

NOTEBOOK

The best way to think about OneNote and how it works is to try and take the concept of the 'notebook' as literal as possible. I like to start by imaging that OneNote is like a giant binder. It's in this binder that I have all my 'notebooks.'

The notebooks are where you start on OneNote. When you open the program for the first time you will find a blank screen with the option to create your first notebook. Again, thinking literally as each notebook will or should be dedicated to one subject. So if you are a student, your first notebook might be for history. Create the notebook and label it as such.

The beautiful thing about OneNote is that there is no limit to how many notebooks you can create. As you have 15gigabytes of free storage one OneDrive, the amount that you can create is near limitless. It really comes to to your own personal preference.

SECTIONS

As soon as you create your first notebook a blank page will appear. At the top left of this page you will see a small tab labelled 'section.' Again, thinking literally, this section is best thought of as a combined grouping of pages in a notebook; usually grouped by theme or subject matter. If this is your history notebook, than this section might be on Alexander the Great.

As with the notebook, there is no limit to how many sections you create. By clicking on the tab you can rename the section to keep it clear as to what the theme of that section is. And if you create an abundance, you can then group sections together, again under theme or idea. OneNote is all about making organisation as easy as possible.

PAGES

The final step to setting up your notebook is the 'pages.' This the first time you will notice OneNote really stepping up its game from Word.

Now that you have your section created, you will look to the left hand side where a column has appeared. In this column it should say 'Untitled Page.' The beauty of OneNote is that there is no limit as to how long you want each page. It all comes down to organisation.

So, if this section is on Alexander the Great. This first page might be about his four major battles. You can thus label the page as such and arrange all your notes about his battles just on this page. You can then create another page about his policies. That page will be entirely dedicated to that topic, and so on. Each time you find new information, you can flip between the pages and add it to the relevant one.

By now you should be starting to see how simple and effective OneNote can be. But that's only the beginning.

Personalisation

One final thing you are going to want to do is personalise your notebooks and sections. Again this is simple to do and usually done as a means to make your work more organised and accessible.

With OneNote you can personalise everything from the colour of you notebook (this option is presented when you first create a new notebook) to the colour of each section. You can also choose if you want each page to be lined, drawn up as a grid or just a blank page. And to take it even further, templates are available to add a flair to the background of each page too, such as flowers drawings and doodles.

OneNote is dedicated to making this working space as personalised and adaptable to your needs as possible.

Chapter Three: Taking Notes

Typing And Writing

TYPING

To type on OneNote is the exact same process that you would do it on Word. You literally click anywhere and type. The key to these feature though is the use of the word 'anywhere.' Unlike word, where your typing is bound by invisible margins and rulers, in OneNote you can click and type anywhere on the page.

Doing this will create a small container that expands as you continue to type. The reason for this container is that once the note is written, you can pick it up and move it anywhere on the page – or to any section of the notebook, or any other notebook. For note taking purposes this means that you don't have to be aware of where the note it being written in comparison to others. It's once you have finished making the notes that you can move and pair them with similar ones.

WRITING

If typing isn't your thing, OneNote allows for users to physically write and take notes by hand. Now, if you have a tablet that allows you use a pen on the screen, than all the better. If not than that's OK too.

A tab called 'draw,' is located at the top of the OneNote screen and in here you will find options for everything from line thickness to colour. The real beauty of OneNote though comes in its ability to transcribe the drawing once you are done.

If you have written, using a pen, OneNote will be able to convert this into typed text, making it easier on the eye and neater on the page. One quick note though, the transcribe isn't always perfect, so it's always worth checking again afterwards.

Pictures

Importing pictures into OneNote couldn't be simpler. In the 'Insert' tab you will see an 'Insert Picture,' option. Click this, open the relevant file and that's that. Just like with a container the picture can be picked up, moved and resized as you see fit.

One more cool function in regards to pictures. If there is a word in the picture, this word is actually searchable. So if you have saved a picture of a recipe for pie and later you search the word 'pie' than this recipe should come up.

Voice Records

Another great feature of OneNote is its ability to audio record. The process is rather simple too, all you need do is hit the 'Audio

Recording' button, found in the 'Insert' tab, and it begins to record automatically.

This will then appear as an audio file in the relevant section and page.

There is one other great feature about this audio function that needs to be mentioned and that is that the audio is actually searchable. So let's say that the word 'dog,' is spoken and recorded. The user can then type the word 'dog,' into the search bar and the audio file will pop up.

Videos

Note: The following information applies to OneNote 2016 only.

OneNote is literally a do-all program. The team at Microsoft have made it there mission to make the gathering an organising of notes as simple and effective as possible. No where else is this more evident than its ability to play video.

Say you find a great Youtube video that goes perfectly with the notes you are trying to make. All you need do it copy the page link to the video and paste it onto the page. It will then appear as a regular Youtube video that is watch-able on the page. You don't need to open the web browser again as OneNote does it all for you.

Tags

Tagging is a very important aspect of OneNote that should be utilised where possible. In the 'Home' tab you will see an entire section dedicated to tags. What these are are little pictures that represent features of note taking. For example, a light-bulb represents an idea you might have for later, where a check mark represents something you need to do.

All you need do is click and drag the tag to each relevant note in order to help it stand out more.

Another great feature, and a recent addition as of 2016, is the ability to search the tags. Next to the add tag location you will see a small icon labelled as 'Find Tags.' clicking on this will bring up a menu that lists all the tags you have used and where to find them.

Grids, Tables And Equations

Grids and tables can be made just like in a word document. And then it too can be picked up and moved. The unique thing about OneNote (2016 version only) is that it then allows you to convert this table or gird into an excel spreadsheet. This will then allow you do use it in excel. From here you can convert the information into any number of graphs and charts as excel allows.

OneNote also has a very simple calculator function. Again, in the 'Insert tab,' you will see an option for 'equations.' This creates a small dialogue box for you to type simple equations into.

Webpages And Hyperlinks

First thing is first. hyperlinks can be copied and pasted into OneNote. It's simple and reasonably effective. But there is a better way to store the information see on a webpage for later use.

The first thing you will need to do this is download the add-on Web Clipper (see Chapter Five). Downloaded, this add-on should insert itself into your taskbar (this varies depending on the web browser that you are using).

Now, once you are on the page that you wish to add to OneNote, simply hit the clipper button. This will redirect you to a new menu which will give you the option of either inserting the whole page into OneNote, clipping just a fragment of the page yourself, or whether you want the clipper to do it for you. If for example you are clipping a page with a food recipe on it, the clipper function will convert the page so that only the recipe and photo of the food is showing.

The final product will then be downloaded to your default notebook and all you need do is move it to the relevant section and page.

Chapter Four: Working With Others

Sharing Your Notebook

Having notes for yourself is all well and good, but sometimes you might want to share these notes with somebody, or better yet you might want someone to add to them. If this were a physical notebook you could rip the page out, hand it over and then take it back when they are done. Although you can't exactly do that, what you are able to do is even better.

In the top right corner of your notebook you will see a little icon of a man with a plus symbol next to him. Click this and the sharing options come up. The options are as follows, Invite people to notebook, copy link to notebook and send page.

Inviting people to notebook allows for the individual to open up your notebook from their own device. When you select this feature you will also see the option of allowing them to edit the notebook or not. Sometime you may want their input, other times you may just want them to see your work.

Copy link to notebook allows you to send a hyperlink to the person in question. They can then copy this into their web-browser and the notebook will pop up. That is if they have a OneNote account.

And finally, the send page feature is exactly as it sounds. You can send a page to a college or friend for them to look at. But it should be noted that sections cannot be sent or shared. You can either share the entire notebook or one page at a time.

Passwords And Locks

The issue with not being able to share a section means that quiet often you will need to share an entire notebook with a person. If there is personal information in here that you don't want anyone else to see, you can simply lock that information; essentially blotting it out.

The password protection function applies to entire sections of your notebook. To implement one is a very straight forward process. Make sure that you have the correct section open. Then, under the 'Review' tab you will see the option for 'Password Protection.' Choose a password and remember it. If you loose your password there is no way of getting back in. Just like if you loose the key to your lock.

Chapter Five: 2016 Features

New Features

With every new release of a platform or program comes inevitable upgrades. The extent of these upgrades is of course dependent on how much needed to be fixed in the first place. As OneNote 2013 was a rather complete product, there are only a few new features added, making it relatively the same.

CLIPPING TOOL

This is probably the biggest improvement that OneNote has made. Previously, when clipping webpages to your notebook, the only way to do this was to clip the entire page. This meant that you were left with a huge, messy chunk of info that you didn't want or need.

Now, with the 2016 release, you have the option of clipping the page and choosing the section that you want. The clipping tool also has the options of reformatting the page for you. So for example if you clip a webpage with a recipe on it, the clipper tool will provide you with a nice, clean layout for which to import this recipe into your notebook.

NEW ADD-ONS

There are a whole host of new add-ons that you can download to help maximise your OneNote experience. I will be going over a few of the better ones in Chapter Five.

TAGS

Another key feature is that the tags are now searchable. In the 2013 version, although you could still use tags, you were unable to search for them later on. This made them all but useless. Now though, lets say you tag something as an 'Idea,' you can later look up all the 'Idea' tags you have.

VIDEOS

The ability to insert complete and watch-able videos from Vimeo and Youtube into a page is a new development.

EMAIL YOURSELF

One cool new feature is the ability to send your OneNote account emails directly. This is extremely convenient for if you're at work, or somewhere that you are unable to log onto your OneNote. Simply email and add the note to the proper section later.

IMPORTING EXCEL

As spoken about in Chapter Two, Excel spreadsheets can be created inside of OneNote. This is a new feature for the 2016 version.

Platform Variations

The two major operating systems that you will be using when operating OneNote are Mac and Windows. Of course, as this is a windows product, the windows version works best. But this is only in small circumstances. For the majority of the features, you will find that they work exactly the same. Below are the few variances you may come across.

PASSWORD LOCK

Although this isn't a feature that is relegated to solely the windows version, there have been reports that the lock feature doesn't always work when being run through a Mac. Again, this won't always be the case but may happen every now and then.

TAGGING

Although you can indeed use tags in both Windows and Mac, the tagging features in Windows are infinity better. The reason for this is that in Windows you can search you tags, where in Mac you can't. This makes the tags almost a redundant feature when using Mac.

AUDIO RECORD

Again, the audio record feature does word in both Mac and Windows. However, the ability to search spoken words is a feature only found in Windows.

Chapter Six: Add-ons

The great thing about OneNote is that it doesn't stop at the downloaded program. Microsoft knows that no user is the same, all wanting different things for different reasons. As such, there are dozens of different add-ons that can be downloaded to help personalise the One Note experience for you.

Below are a list of a few of my personal favourites.

WEB CLIPPER

This is a must have add-on for any OneNote user. Although I've already mentioned it previously, I'm going to again because it really is vital for anyone serious about their note taking.

Web Clipper is a free download that allows the user to clip pages from the web and import them into their notebook. And more than that it has the added features (as of 2016) to clip the page specifically, so you only take the information that you want. This is an add-on that you will use time and time again.

ONETASTIC

The first thing you should do when you start using OneNote is download OneTastic. On its own it doesn't do much, but it what it lets you do later on that's important. OneTastic will give the user access to dozens of macros and add-ons that will really help spice up your OneNote use and ensure that you get the most out of it.

MACROS

Once you have OneTastic, you will be able to start using Macros. Macro's are like shortcuts that make formatting that little bit easier. Below are a few of the more popular ones:

- Sort Pages – Helps you sort pages in each section by name

- Number of Pages – Displays the number of pages in current sections

- Set all pictures to background – this will let you set the pictures as background images. This allow you to write over them.

- No Spell Check – This removes all the spelling and grammar lines that appear when you make an error.

These are only a few examples too. There are dozens of options for you too choose from.

ONECALENDER

You'll need OneTastic to download this but it is worth it. OneCalander can be used as either its own icon on your desktop or inserted into the taskbar of your OneNote. What it is is a calender display of your history in OneNote. It will show you where you have recently been, notebooks, sections and pages, allowing you to keep better track of your activities.

OFFICE LENS

If you hate taking notes than this one is for you. Office Lens is an app you can download on your phone or Ipad that is used for taking pictures specifically for OneNote. Or, to be more specific, it's used to take pictures of whiteboards and printed documents. The reason this is needed is that OneLens can then sharpen and import the image into OneNote so it looks like it was typed, rather than being a direct, messy looking image.

ONENOTE PUBLISHER FOR WORDPRESS

If you're a blog writer who does the majority of their writing in OneNote than this is a great add-on to save you time. Rather than having to manually import your writings, piecemeal, into your blog site, OneNote Publisher for Wordpress allows you to import the entire page in one go.

Chapter Seven: 125 Tips and Tricks

1) Deactivating The Snap Grid

When you try and move an item or text on OneNote it follows invisible guidelines, helping move it into place. This is known as snapping. To remove this function do the following

Hold the ALT button down while moving the object

2) Moving A Container Using Your Keyboard Only

- Select the container

- Right click to open the context menu

- Select the 'Move' command or press M

- Now you can use your arrows to move containers

3) Splitting Containers

Although it's nice to have all your work split up into separate containers so you can move them around at will, what do you do when you want to split the information into separate containers?

- Select/highlight all the content that you want to move

- Press and hold the left mouse button and drag. They will form a new container

4) Merging containers

- Hold your mouse pointer at the quadruple-dot title bar source container. A four sided mouse container will appear

- Hold SHIFT and left click with the mouse. Drag and drop the source container in with the new container.

5) Forcing The Creation Of A New Container

Often when you try and create multiple new containers at once, as a means of setting up your layout before entering the information, you will find OneNote merging these containers together.

To avoid this, make sure that you double click for the creation of each new one. This will confirm and save its creation.

6) Splitting A Table Horizontally

- Click in the cell or the multiple cells you wish to split

- In the LAYOUT tab you will see the 'Table Tools.'

- In 'Merge Group,' click 'Split Cells'

- Enter the amount of columns and rows you wish to split

7) Inserting Space Horizontally And Vertically

If you need free space in between containers but don't want to have to rearrange the whole page, than this feature is perfect for widening those gaps.

- Open the INSERT tab

- There you will see an 'Insert Space,' function

- Select where you wish to insert the space. Simply drag the arrow across until you have enough room

- Although the arrow is pictured as being vertical, it can also be used horizontally as well

8) Download Macros

One tip that I can't emphasise enough is to check the Macro's out after you download the app OneTastic. There are so many to choose from and many of the problems you may be experience, especially in regards to formatting, can be solved through Macro's

9) Limiting The Page Size

The unlimited size of pages in OneNote can be a hassle when it comes to printing. If you want to pre-empt this and limit how big you can make a page, it's very very simple to do.

- In the VIEW tab select the 'Paper Size,' function

- To the right a new 'task pane' gets created where you are free to either create your own margins or choose more traditional ones.

10) Moving Pages Including Subpages

OneNote allows for it user to very easily move pages around to get them in the order that you like. What's more, you can also have subpages coming off your main page. The only issue with this is when you move the main page later, the subpages won't follow. There is a way around this

- First, collapse all subpages. This means that only the title of the main page should be showing.

- Only once you have done this are you able to move all pages, including the subpages, in one go.

11) Removing Empty Space

Much like you can create space, you can all limit it too. This again saves you having to rearrange your entire page layout.

- Open the INSERT tab

- There you will see an 'Insert Space,' function.

- Select where you wish to remove the space. Simply drag the arrow inwards, eliminating the space. It works exactly the same as if you were creating space.

12) Panning A Page To See Your Work

- On the ribbon select the DRAW tab

- In TOOLS click 'Panning Hand'

- Use your mouse on the page now to drag any way you would like

- Press ESC to finish the pan

13) Moving PDF Files, Including Annotations

When you add multiple containers, including PDF files to a page, they may seem like they are all part of the one grouping. But they are not. If you move one, the others will not follow. This is simple to fix.

When moving a group of objects, make sure that you use CTRL + click, holding and dragging the mouse to select all.

14) Locking The Position of PDF Documents

- Right click on the PDF and select 'Set Picture As Background.'

- It should be noted that this also allows for you to place other containers over the PDF now as it is technically part of the canvas.

15) Colouring A Text Container

- This can be a great way to distinguish different notes on the page

- First, type the text you want.

- Next CTRL + A (select all)

- Next go to the INSERT tab and select 'Table.'

- This will put the text you have created inside a single cell of a table.

- You can then easily colour the table and this will also colour the background of your text.

16) Adding A Coloured Border Around An Image or Text

- Right click on the text box, container, or image

- Select 'Format' and click the 'Colours and Lines,' button

- Under 'Line,' choose the colour

17) White Grid On A Coloured Background

- First, open a new page

- Next select the VIEW tab and go to 'Page Colour.'

- Once you have the desired colour, choose 'Rule Lines.'

- Click the small drop down menu option to change the colour of the grid lines

18) Applying The Same Background Colour To Multiple Pages

I find the best way to do this is to create a template of the page that you want so that you can access it later.

- First, create a new page

- Next select the VIEW tab and go to 'Page Colour.'

- Now, over on the 'Pages' task pane click the small arrows to activate the drop down menu.

- Select the 'More Template Choice and Options.'

- At the bottom of this task pane is a small link to 'Save Current Page as Template.'

19) Basic Equations And The Finding Symbols

- In the INSERT tab you will see a button for 'Equations.' Selecting this will open a new container to type said equations

- Now, in order to insert actual symbols for your equation, right click on the container then hit 'Edit,' then 'Emoji and Symbol'

- Next click 'Math Symbols.'

- Double click the symbol you wish to use.

20) AutoCorrect Phrase Expansion

This is a simple one and usually used for speed and personal preference. But sometimes that standard AutoCorrect functions don't suit your needs. These are easy to solve.

- Select the FILE tab, then 'Options,' then 'Proofing,' and finally 'AutoCorrect Options.'

- In here you can change any settings you want and even add your own words if need be.

21) Restoring The Original Image Size

Often an image that you import into OneNote won't be the original size that it was taken in. This is on account of scaling and the resolution that you took the image in.

To solve this, and restore it to its original glory, right click on the image and you will see the option for 'Restore to Original Size.' Just be careful when you do this as it may ruin your layout.

22) Highlight Text The Easy Way

- A very simple shortcut to highlight text is to press CTRL + ALT + H

23) Having Two Windows Open At Once

This is a great one if you're working on two project simultaneously and don't want to keep going back and forth between two separate windows.

- Start by opening two OneNote windows. You can do this by hitting CTRL + M

- Now that you have two OneNote windows open, you should be able to go to the task bar and see the two separate OneNote windows

- While on window one hit CTRL and right click on the tab for the second OneNote window.

- Select the 'Show Windows Side by Side,' option.

24) Start OneNote In Docked Mode

Docking is the process by which OneNote will always be open and accessible. If you have say, a web browser open, OneNote will be squashed to the side like a task pane, but still able to be used.

- CTR + ATL + D should dock this for you

- If not, you can also go through your QAT customisation

- Right click on the QAT

- Click 'Customise Quick Access Toolbar

- Select 'All Commands'

- In the 'Choose Commands From List,' click 'Dock to Desktop'

25) Distraction Free Editing And Presenting

When you open your OneNote, there is a lot going on. There's the task bars, ribbons, section and page counters...it's all very distracting. There is a simple way to get rid of all of this so that all you have to deal with is a blank page. Simply hit F11 and everything but the canvas will disappear.

26) Why Your Custom Paragraph Spacings Don't Work

This is a pretty common problem. Basically you need to realise that OneNote isn't Word. In Word you can type any number into the alignment spacings and it will process the new alignment for you. In OneNote you need to be more precise. If you don't type the spacing down to the decimal point than it won't work for you.

27) Put A Visual QuickNote On Your Screen

These are kind of like sticky notes and they're great for reminding you of your upcoming tasks.

- Click the VIEW tab

- Now select 'New Quick Note.'

- Type your note

- You can move these anywhere on your screen by dragging and dropping.

28) Create A QuickNote When OneNote Isn't Running

- On your keyboard press WINDOWS + N

- Type your note into the small window

29) Review All Your QuickNotes

- Select the name of your current notebook

- At the bottom of the notebook list you should see 'QuickNotes'

- Open this too see your quick notes as relevant to that notebook.

30) Grouping Sections Together

- Right click anywhere in the notebook header

- Select the 'New Section Group,' option

- Enter the name of the group and press 'Enter,'

- You can now click and drag the sections you want into that group

31) Managing Section Groups

- If you want to see all the sections in your section group, click the 'Navigate to Parent Section Group,' which is the small green arrow to the left of the section groups name

- To delete a section group, right click on the tab and hit 'Delete.' You will then be prompted as to whether you want to delete individual sections too

32) Moving A Notebook To Another Location

This is one for people not using OneNote 2016. As of 2016 you can open your notebook on any device.

- Open the notebook you wish to share and select 'File,' then 'Share.'

- Now choose the drive that you want to move the notebook too

- Click 'Move Notebook.'

- Now, when you open OneNote on another device you should be able to go in and find this notebook.

33) Renaming A Notebook

- First, sign out of OneNote

- Now open OneDrive and navigate towards the notebook you wish to edit, found in the 'Documents' folder

- Move the mouse pointer over the notebook and click. This will allow you to select the small check-box that appears

- Now click 'Manage,' and 'Rename.'

34) Deleting A Notebook

Deleting a notebook from OneNote can't be done in the program as it is backed up online, not on your computer. It needs to be done at the source.

- First, sign out of OneNote

- Now open OneDrive and navigate towards the notebook you wish to edit, found in the 'Documents' folder

- Move the mouse pointer over the notebook and click. This will allow you to select the small checkbox that appears

- Now click 'Manage,' and 'Delete.'

- Be wary, this is permanent.

35) Creating Custom Tags

- Under the 'HOME' tab scroll across to the 'Tag Menu'

- Look for the small arrow drop down menu option

- Click on this and it will show you the long list of available tags.

- At the bottom of this list is the 'Custom Tag' option

- Here you can select symbols, names and colours. One tip is to hashtag your custom tag. This will allow you to search for it later

36) Searching Tags

As of the 106 version, tags are searchable. This means that if you create a 'To Do' tag, you can search for it and all others later on. Very convenient.

- Open the HOME tab

- Select the 'Find Tags' icon

- In here you can search tags. If there are too many you can narrow the search scope by clicking 'Search' in the drop down menu.

37) Using Multiple Accounts

If you use multiple accounts (besides the Microsoft one you logged in on) but want them all to have access to your one OneNote account, it's pretty simple to do.

- Once you have OneNote open, select 'Settings.'

- In 'Settings,' open 'Accounts.'

- Now click the 'Add Account' option

38) Remove Accounts

- Open the 'Settings' side pane

- Down the bottom you should see the name of the account that is currently open

- In the 'Account' pop up that appears, select 'Sign Out.'

39) Moving Sections and pages Using Drag And Drop

This is an exceptionally easy one. All you need to do to move pages and sections is select them and drag and drop them in the new notebook/section that you want. Just realise that this is moving, not copying them

40) Scrolling Between Pages In A Section

- CTRL + PG UP or CTRL + PG DOWN will scroll through the pages rather than having you need to click on each on.

41) Sorting Pages Alphabetically/Numerically

I wanted to add this just to clear the argument up. The easiest way to sort pages is to download the Macro for it. Many different Macros exist that will do this for you. Otherwise, doing it manually is the only way

42) Creating A Page In The Middle Of A Pages List

Again, the only way to do this is to do it manually. Create a page as you would any other time and then drag and drop.

43) Making A Page Title Invisible

- Go to the VIEW tab

- Select 'Hide Page Title.'

44) Swap Page List From Right To Left

- Go to FILE tab

- Then open 'Options'

- Next open the 'Display' section and you will see a little box that should read 'Page Tabs Appear On The Left.'

- Remove the check from this box

45) Creating Pages Without The Date And Time Stamp

- First, create a new page

- Then highlight the automatically created time and date that appears in the top corner

- Now, over on the 'Pages' task pane click the small arrows to activate the drop down menu.

- Select the 'More Template Choice and Options.'

- At the bottom of this task pane is a small link to 'Save Current Page as Template.'

- When you save it the option to make this page the default will appear. Select this option and save.

46) Editing Page Templates

- First thing is first, add a new page

- Next go to the VIEW tab and choose 'Paper Size'

- Then add any content that you want to appear on this page e.g. you can change the colour, add a picture and set it as a background, add rulers and margins etc

- Now, over on the 'Pages' task pane click the small arrows to activate the drop down menu.

- Select the 'More Template Choice and Options.'

- At the bottom of this task pane is a small link to 'Save Current Page as Template.'

47) Setting Rule Lines As Default Page Layout

- In the VIEW tab select the 'Rule Lines' option.

- Here you can choose what types of rulers and lines you would like on your page

- Now, over on the 'Pages' task pane click the small arrows to activate the drop down menu.

- Select the 'More Template Choice and Options.'

- At the bottom of this task pane is a small link to 'Save Current Page as Template.'

- When you save it the option to make this page the default will appear. Select this option and save.

48) Opening A Page At Windows Start Menu

- Right click on the page title and select 'Pin to Start.'

- It automatically pins itself, with the same name.

49) Creating Desktop Shortcuts To Pages

- Right click on the title of the page and select 'Pin to Start.'

- Once it's in the Start Menu, pick it up and drag it to the desktop

- This will create a thumbnail that when selected will automatically open that page in OneNote

50) Pin A Notebook To The Start Menu/Task Bar

- Just like with a page, all you need do is right click on the title of the notebook and select 'Pin to Start.'

- The link is created automatically for you

- You can then select if you want it pinned to your task bar in the same manner

51) Viewing Your Version History

If you want to see every single edit you have made to a note, you can do it quiet simply. Under the HISTORY tab you can use the 'Recent Edits' menu to select certain times and dates to view what changes you made.

52) Displaying Your Most Recent Notes

This is a handy one if you want to see when you made certain changes.

- Go to the HISTORY tab

- Select 'Recent Edits'

- Pick the date range you wish to work with

- Here you can fiddle with the range of edits and dates you wish to see

53) Search Phrases, Not Just Single Words

This is simple one. When you use the search function, simply put quotation marks around the phrase you wish to search

54) In-Page Table Of Contents

There is unfortunately no way of doing this with just the simple OneNote program. A Macro does exist though called 'TOC In Current Page.' It's a free download and works wonderfully.

55) Sharing Notes

This is the best way to invite other users to view or co-author a note for you; or to just take a look

- Open the notebook that you want to share (or the specific page)

- Click 'File,' then 'Share', then 'Share With People.'

- Alternately you should be able to see a small symbol in the top left of a man with a 'plus' sign next to him. Selecting this will do the same thing.

- In the column under 'Share,' make sure 'Invite People' is selected

- In the 'To Box,' type the email address of the person you wish to share with

- You can also add a note to go with the delivery if need be

56) Removing Notebooks Shared By You

- Click 'File,' then 'Share,' then 'Invite People.'

- Under 'Shared With,' right click the persons name

- You can either remove them completely or change the options by which they see your work

57) Removing Notebooks On OneDrive For Business

This is the same process that you will go through when deleting a notebook from your personal drive. The only difference is that you will need access to your business' OneDrive account

- First, sign out of OneNote

- Now open OneDrive and navigate towards the notebook you wish to edit, found in the 'Documents' folder

- Move the mouse pointer over the notebook and click. This will allow you to select the small check-box that appears

- Now click 'Manage,' and 'Delete.'

- Be wary, this is permanent.

58) Send Screenshots Of Your Screen To OneNote

- Hit the Windows + S key to take a quick screen grab

- You can then send this automatically into OneNote.

- It will go to your default page so you will have to move it later

59) Collapsing And Expanding Task Pane Group Headings

This is a relatively simple one. All you need to do is click the small minus sign next to the group heading. It behaves the same way for single task panes too.

60) Repositioning The Notebook Bar

- Go to the FILE tab

- Then open 'Options'

- Next open the 'Display' section and there you will see an option to move the notebook bar.

- Remove the check from this box

61) Turning Off The Mini-Tool Bar

- Click the 'Microsoft Office Button' and click 'OneNote Options'

- Click 'Popular,' and then 'Top Options for Working With Powerpoint

- Clear the 'Show Mini Tool Bar on Selection' check box

62) Resizing The Toolbar

- On the toolbar press CTRL + SPACEBAR. This will display the toolbar options

- Click the 'Size' command and press ENTER

- Use the arrows to adjust the size

63) Moving The Toolbar

- On the toolbar press CTRL + SPACEBAR. This will display the toolbar options

- Click the 'move' command and press ENTER

- Use the arrows to move it where you would like

64) Adding And Removing Commands From The Quick Access Toolbar That Are On The Ribbon (QAT)

- On the ribbon, click the appropriate tab or group to display the command that you want to add to the QAT

- Right click on the command then click 'Add to Quick Access Toolbar'

65) Keyboard Shortcuts To Access The Quick Access Toolbar Options

- Press ALT

- Then press F to open the FILE tab

- Press T to open the OPTIONS tab

- Select the 'Quick Access Toolbar'

- Press TAB to move into the QAT

- Press C to open the drop down feature list

- Now add the features you want.

66) Positioning The Quick Access Toolbar Under The Ribbon

Click the small arrows in the top corner of the QAT and in the list select 'Show Below Ribbon.'

67) Resetting the Quick Access Toolbar

- Right click on the QAT

- Click the 'Customise the Quick Access Toolbar' option

- Now click 'Reset Default' and select 'Reset Only Quick Access Toolbar

68) Adding Command To The Quick Access Toolbar That Isn't On The Ribbon

- Right click on the QAT

- Click 'Customise Quick Access Toolbar'

- Select 'More Commands'

- In the 'Choose Commands From List,' click 'Commands Not On The Ribbon.'

69) Removing Commands From The Quick Access Toolbar

- Right click the command you wish to remove

- Then click 'Remove From Quick Access toolbar

70) Can You Add Galleries To The Quick Access Toolbar?

As of right now there is no way to do this that I am aware of. I added it just so you would be aware of the problem too

71) Change The Order Of Commands On The Quick Access Toolbar

- Right click on the QAT

- Click 'Customise Quick Access Toolbar'

- Under 'Customise Quick Access Toolbar,' click the command you wish to move and click the 'Move Up,' or 'Move Down,' command

72) Group the Commands On The Quick Access Toolbar

This one separates the commands on the QAT, so they're easier on the eye/

- Right click on the QAT

- Click 'Customise Quick Access Toolbar'

- In the 'Choose Commands From,' list, click 'Popular Demands.'

- Click 'Separator,' and then click 'Add'

- To place the separator where you want click 'Move Up,' or 'Move Down.'

73) Customise the Quick Access Toolbar Using The Options Command

- Click the FILE tab

- Under HELP click 'Options'

- Click the 'Quick Access Toolbar,'

- Makes the changes

74) Multi-Level Undo

This is essentially the ability to go back several steps at once and select which error you wish to go to. Rather than having to go step by step.

- Click the small drop down arrow in the QAT

- Next select 'More Commands'

- Change the 'Choose Commands' option to 'All commands'

- Next scroll down to the 'Undo' command and select 'Add'

- Now, when you select 'Undo' you will have the drop down option of going back several steps at once.

75) Customising The Ribbon

- Open the FILE tab

- Under HELP, click 'options.'

- Click 'Customise Ribbon.'

76) Resetting The Ribbon Back To Default

- Open OneNote OPTIONS

- There you will see a 'Customise Ribbon' button

- Open this and hit the 'Reset' button in the bottom right

77) Relocating Task Panes

The task pane is a multi-purpose window pane appearing on the right hand side of the page.

In the task pane press CTRL + SPACEBAR. This will display a list of additional commands

Now press the down arrow to select the 'move' command

Use the arrow keys to move the task pane

78) Resizing Task Panes

- In the task pane press CTRL + SPACEBAR. This will display a list of additional commands

- Use the DOWN ARROW to select SIZE. Select

- Use the arrow keys to adjust the size

79) Setting The Default Font

It's usually set to size 11 Calibri. If this isn't your thing than it's worth a change.

- Go to the FILE tab and select 'Options'

- In the OneNote Options dialogue box, 'Default Font' select the size and style you would like.

80) Exporting Files To Another File Format

- In the file menu click 'Save As'

- Click OneNote 2016 Section (*.One) in the select file format area

- Click 'Save As'

81) Moving The Cache File Folder

The cache folder is where OneNote sores backup files.

- Click 'File,' then 'Options,' and then 'Save and Backup'

- Under 'Save', in the paths list, click 'Backup Folder' and then select 'Modify.'

- In the 'Select Folder' dialogue box, navigate to the location where you want OneNote to store backup files and click 'Select.'

82) Working Offline

This is simple to do. Basically OneNote syncs to OneDrive automatically as you work. If at any point your internet access drops out, than you can continue to work. The next time you have online access, OneNote will re-sync and everything will be saved.

83) Discovering The OneNote Version Number

Knowing this may come in handy when you want to find out what features you have and what you may be missing.

To locate your version number, simply click the 'Start Menu' button, scroll through the 'Apps Menu' until you find 'Microsoft

Office.' Then click the down arrow to the right and you should see what version number you have.

84) Hiding The Author Initials

This is a simple one if you want to keep your work a little more private. Simple go the HISTORY tab and select 'Hide Author.'

85) Adding A Speak Feature To OneNote

- In the QAT, select the drop down menu

- Open the 'Customize Quick Access Toolbar' feature

- Select 'More Commands'

- Where it says, 'Choose Commands From,' select 'All Commands'

- Scroll to the bottom where the 'Speak' option is

- Add this to the QAT. Now when you highlight text and press this command it will 'speak' it for you

86) Bookmark Voice Recordings

- First, you have to record something. To do this go to the INSERT tab and hit the 'Audio Record' button

- Later, when you are listen to the recording you can use the 'Bookmark' function. This automatically pinpoints sections of the audio for you to listen back to later

87) Search Audio Notes Like Normal Text

One great feature of the 106 version is that if you have a clear audio recording, you can search for specific words and phrases said in it. OneNote will find them and give you the time code.

- First, make sure that your audio recording is clear and precise

- Go into 'Options,' and open 'Audio and Video'

- Down the bottom, under 'Audio Search,' tick the box to enable this feature

- Although it isn't perfect, it still works very well

88) Adding Video To OneNote

If you have OneNote 2016 than this could not be easier. All you have to do, quite literally, is copy a video URL and past it. You can then watch the video in OneNote itself without having to reopen the browser.

89) Import Using The Print Driver

This is a good one when you have a file that can't be imported from OneNote. This is usually for older version as 2016 can import almost any file.

- Open the file with the appropriate program e.g. Microsoft Word for a word doc.

- Open FILE and then 'Print'

- In the print dialogue box, select the 'Send to OneNote' option

- Then hit print

- This should go to your default notebook

90) Scan To OneNote

The easiest way to do this it to download the Windows Scan for Windows 10. This will allow you to scan a file onto your computer into a format that is compatible with OneNote.

91) Email To Onenote

The ability to email your OneNote from any server is a feature that is reserved only for OneNote2016.

- When you create a OneNote account you will have the options of creating an email address –

- Next you will be presented with the options to choose where these emails go i.e which notebook they go into.

- Now you can email your notebook from any email server you choose

92) Printing PDF Documents To OneNotes

If you have the 2016 version than this won't apply to you. The 2016 version can import any file.

- Open the PDF in Adobe Reader or a similar program.

- Click FILE and then select 'Print.'

- Select 'Send to OneNote'

- Click 'Print' and this should send the file to OneNote in the correct form.

93) Can You Print An Entire Notebook?

The bad news is that no you can't. The idea behind OneNote is that it's a digital notebook so you shouldn't ever need to print anything. But, sometimes that just isn't an option. So OneNote allows the printing of single pages at a time.

94) Converting Handwriting

If you have a Tablet or an equvilent device that you can actually draw onto, than this gives you the ability to take notes by hand, directly into OneNote and convert it to text later.

- Open the DRAW tab

- Choose the 'Lasso Select' option

- Drag the pointer over the hand written text.

- Next, in the DRAW tab again, select 'Ink to Text.'

95) Sending Handwritten Notes To Word

The best way to do this is to convert the handwritten words to text first. Then you will be able to send them to word without a problem with conversion.

- Open the DRAW tab

- Choose the 'Lasso Select' option

- Drag the pointer over the hand-written text.

- Next, in the DRAW tab again, select 'Ink to Text.'

96) Pull Text From An Image

Yep, you can literally pull text from an image as in, a jpeg that you insert which has words can be pulled and edited.

- First, make sure there is actual text in the image

- Right click on the image and select 'Copy Text From Picture.'

- You can then paste that text back into your blank canvas and edit as normal text.

97) Search For Words Found In Pictures

One great feature in OneNote 2016 is its ability to now search words in PDF photos and pictures. It doesn't work every time but the majority of the time it will locate these words in the search bar.

98) Hyperlinking Another Page To Your Notes (V1)

This is perfect if you are working on a note that is also relevant to another page. You can simply link that page into the current notes you are taking.

- Types the sentence that you wish to link

- Next, inside the container, type the name of the relevant page and enclose the name inside of the '[[]]' symbols. Like brackets.

- For example, to link Page One to this note I would simply write 'Note [[Page One]] and that would create a hyperlink straight to the page.

- This can be done to a notebook that you aren't even working in. as long as the page name is spelt correctly.

99) Hyperlinking Another Page To Your Notes (V2)

- Right click on the destination where you want the link to appear. From here you should be able to choose the 'Copy Link To...' option

- Then go to the text you wish to link, select it and hit CTRL + K

- When the address bar pops up, paste the link into it. This should create a link between the two

100) Link To A Website

This is the creation of a hyperlink that, when clicked, will open a corresponding page in a web browser.

- Select the text you want to link the website

- Press CTRL + K

- This will create a link address box

- Simple add the URL from the wessite and you will have created a hyperlink to the webpage

101) Link Webpages Back Into OneNote

- The easiest way to do this is to copy the URL and past it directly onto the page that you are working on. This will create a link.

- OR you can copy a slab of text and paste it into the page. This will automatically bring with it the URL, as well as the text

102) Send Or Pass A Link To A Page

- Create the note

- In the top right hand corner of the page you will see a small icon of a man with a + next to him

- Hit 'Get a Link'

103) Sending Outlook Emails To OneNote

This is only for people with an older version of OneNote as the new version is Outlook compatible

- Select the email you wish to send to OneNote

- In the 'Move' group, select 'OneNote

- There will be then be a task pane that asks for you to select the location in OneNote that you wish to email too

- Select the relevant notebook and hit 'OK'

- OneNote will then launch itself automatically

104) Pasting Slides From Powerpoint

- In Powerpoint, open the 'File' menu and select 'Print.'

- Then select the 'Send to OneNote' option along with the slides you wish to import

- Click Print

- These will now be compatible with OneNote

105) Configuring Automatic Backups

By default, OneNote automatically backs your notes up online at regular intervals. But you can also make sure that it back ups into a physical location on your computer Just to be safe.

- Choose 'File' then 'Options

- In the 'OneNote Options,' chose 'Save and Backup,'

- On the right, under 'Save' choose 'Backup Folder,' and then 'Modify.'

- In the 'Select Folder' dialogue box you can choose where you want the files to be backed up to

106) Restoring Backup Files

- Click 'File,' then 'Info,' then 'Open Backups.'

- Double click the folder that you wish to restore and then click 'Open.'

- To restore, right click on either the entire section tab, or open the section and right click on the pages. Then 'Move and Copy.'

- In the 'Move and Copy' dialogue box you can now select where you want these files sent.

107) Backup Using ONEPKG Files

- Select 'File,' then 'Export,' and then 'Notebook

- Now choose the notebook that you wish to export

- This will export the entire notebook to the location of your choosing as a OneNote ONEPKG file

108) Opening ONEPKG Files With Free OneNotes

If you have OneNote installed in your computer than opening the file is as simple as double clicking on it. When you do it will ask you were you want to extract the file too. This just means, where will you be storing the file as you work on it. Choose a file in your hard drive and it will open.

109) Retrieving Deleted Notes From Your Computer

- Open the notebook where you lost the notes

- Click 'File' then 'Info' then 'Backup.'

- In the 'Open Backup,' dialogue box, note the folder names. Each folder represents a name of a notebook that you have created

- Double click the relevant folder, and if the notes are located in their use the 'Move nd Copy' command to put the notes back in their original location

110) Retrieving Deleted Notes Shared Notes

- Open the shared notebook where you lost your notes

- Click 'History,' and then 'Notebook Recycle Bin,'

- If your deleted notes are in their, 'Move and Copy' them. They will return to their original location.

111) Auto-Lock Password Protection Sections

- Open the section that you wish to lock

- Right click on the tab where the section is labelled

- Click the 'Lock Protected Sections' option

- Choose a password

112) Can I Retrieve My Password?

The short and only answer to this is no you cannot. Think of it like a literal lock and key. You lose the key you can't open the lock.

113) Using Multiple Platforms

If you're using the 2016 version (which you should be as it's free) than OneNote works across all platforms. As the storage is not online this makes it easy to jump between them without losing any work.

114) Make And Share To-Do Lists

This is just a great piece of ad vice if you and the people you know all use OneNote. It's an awesome way to keep on top of tasks.

- First thing is first. Make the to-do List.

- When it is done, tag each item with a 'To Do' tag – unchecked

- Then click on 'File' and select 'Share.' - you can share either the page or the link

- That person can now access that page and tick off the 'To Do' items as either of you complete the tasks

115) Embed An Excel Spreadsheet Into OneNote

Again, this is a new feature to the 2016 version

- Start off by creating a grid or table on your page – you can do this through INSERT and then selecting the 'Table' function

- Once the table is created how you would like go to the LAYOUT tab and hit 'Convert to Excel Spreadsheet'

- This will open the table in Excel. Here all the excel features are available and once you are finished taking advantage of them, hit 'Save' and it saves the spreadsheet back into OneNote

116) Insert And ASCII or Unicode Character

- Click where you want the ASCII or Unicode character to go

- Click the INSERT tab, then select 'Symbols,' and then 'More Symbols.'

- In the 'Symbol' box and the 'Font' box, select the one you want

- In the 'From' box click ASCII or Unicode

- Double-click the symbol that you want to insert

117) Four Quick Shortcuts For Adding New Pages To A Section

- Add a new page to the end of the section – CTRL + N

- Add a new page below the current tab as the same level – CTRL + ALT + N

- Add a subpage below the current one – CTRL + ATL + SHIFT + N

- Turn the current page into a subpage – CTRL + Alt +]

118) Basic Editing Shortcuts

- Open a new OneNote window – CTRL + M

- Open a small OneNote window for quick notes – CTRL + SHIFT + M

- Select all items on a page – CTRL + A

- Insert a line break – SHIFT + ENTER

- Open a thesaurus on a selected word – SHIFT + F7

• Bring up the context menu for any selected item – SHIFT + F10

119) Sharing Notes With Outlook Shortcuts

- Create a Today Outlook task – CRTL + SHIFT + 1

- Create a Tomorrow Outlook task – CTRL + SHIST + 2

- Create a This Week Outlook task – CTRL + SHIFT + 3

- Create a Next Week Outlook task – CTRL + SHIFT + 4

- Open the Outlook task – CTRL + SHIFT + K

- Delete the Selected Outlook task – CRTL + SHIFT + O

120) Adding Items To A Page shortcuts

- Insert a document or file – ALT + N, F

- Insert a picture – ALT + N, P

- Insert a picture from a scanner – ALT + N, S

- Insert the current date – ALT + SHIFT + D

- Insert the date and time – ALT + SHIFT + F

- Insert the time – ALT + SHIFT + T

- Start a math equation – ALT + =

- Create a paragraph in the same cell – ALT + ENTER

121) Selecting Notes And Objects Shortcuts

- Select all items on the current page – CTLR + A

- Select to the end of the line – SHIFT + END

- Select the whole line – SHIFT + DOWN ARROW

- Move the selected paragraph – ALT + SHIFT + ARROW

- Move to the beginning of the line – HOME

- Move to the end of the line – END

122) Tagging Notes Shortcuts

- Apply or clear To Do tag – CTRL 1

- Apply or clear Important tag – CTRL 2

- Apply or clear Question tag – CTRL 3

- Apply or clear Remember For Later tag – CTRL 4

- Apply or clear Definition tag – CTRL 5

- Apply or clear a Custom tag – CTRL 6

123) Organising Pages Shortcuts

- Enable or disable full page – F11

- Expand or collapse the tabs of a page group – CTRL + SHIFT + *

- Print the current page – CTRL + P

- Add a new page at the end of the section – CTRL + N

- Go to the next paragraph – CTRL + DOWN ARROW

- Go to the previous paragraph – CTRL + UP ARROW

- Go to the next container – ALT + DOWN ARROW

- Save changes – CTRL + S

124) Organising Notebooks And Sections Shortcuts

- Open OneNote – Windows + SHIFT + N

- Open a notebook – CTRL + O

- Send to OneNote – Windows + N

- Create a new section – CTRL + T

- Open a section – CTRL + ALT + SHIFT + O

- Go the the next section – CTRL + TAB

- Switch to a different Notebook – CTRL + G + ARROW

125) Searching Notes Shortcuts

- Change the search scope – CTRL + E, TAB, SPACE

- Open the search results pane – ALT + O (after searching)

- Search only the current page – CTRL + F

- Dismiss search and return to page – ESC

- While searching current page move to next result – ENTER or F3

www.ingramcontent.com/pod-product-compliance
Lightning Source LLC
Chambersburg PA
CBHW071724170526
45165CB00005B/2148